RASPBERRY PI

*A Step by Step Guide for Beginners to
Program and Set-Up Top 10 Raspberry Pi
Projects + First Steps on Configuration*

Jonathan Cage

Contents

Contents

RASPBERRY PI

The Raspberry Pi is a mini computer that was originally intended for schoolchildren and students. It is therefore very cheap and only costs around 35 euros. This mini-computer enables initial contact with Linux, shell scripting, programming, physical computing and can also be used in productive use. Incidentally, you can learn a lot about the basic functioning of computers with the Raspberry Pi.

The Raspberry Pi was developed due to a decline in the number of applicants for the computer science course at the University of Cambridge. Instead of pure theory, the aim was to upgrade the course with practical applications.

Components required to operate the Raspberry Pi

In addition to the single-board computer, you need a few other components to operate the Raspberry Pi. Since no power supply unit is integrated on the board, an external power adapter with the appropriate voltage and power can be connected to the mini computer via the USB socket. A monitor is required for graphic output. The keyboard and mouse for controlling and operating the device can be connected via USB.

Basically, there is no fixed operating system for the Raspberry Pi. The computer can run with various operating systems via a memory card that is inserted into the existing memory card slot. It is recommended to use the special Linux distribution Raspbian, which is based on Debian Linux. The latest Raspberry models are also compatible with Windows 10. However, a special small device variant of Windows 10 is required.

The different models of the Raspberry Pi

There are numerous different models of the Raspberry Pi. Since the market launch in 2012, the performance of the mini computers has developed significantly. The following versions of the Raspberry Pi are among the best known (most recent versions are mentioned first, as of late 2017):

- Raspberry Pi 3 Model B
- Raspberry Pi 2 Model B
- Raspberry Pi Zero
- Raspberry Pi 1 Model B and B +
- Raspberry Pi 1 model A and A +

In the first generation of devices, ARM CPUs with a clock frequency of 700 megahertz were still installed (ARMv6/32 bit). In the latest model, the Raspberry Pi 3 Model B, an ARMv8 quad-core processor (64 bit) with a clock frequency of 1.2 gigahertz does its job. It has a gigabyte of SDRAM memory. The Raspberry Pi Zero is particularly compact and inexpensive. With its board width of just over 30 instead of 56 millimeters, it occupies a special position among the models. The Pi Zero lacks an Ethernet and FBAS interface. HDMI and USB sockets have been reduced to the mini HDMI and micro USB format.

Expand the Raspberry Pi

The most important features of the Raspberry Pi include its almost unlimited expansion options. The Raspberry Pi can be easily expanded via its integrated USB interface. Devices such as USB cameras, USB memory sticks or USB WLAN and USB surf sticks can be connected there. The only requirement for use is the availability of a suitable driver that is supported by the operating system. In addition to the expansion options via USB interface, expansion boards for the GPIO pin header are available. There is even a separate extension standard for this. It is the HAT standard (Hardware Attached on the Top), which defines, among other things, the dimensions and shape of the expansion boards. This allows a board according to the HAT standard to be attached and attached to the Raspberry Pi. The drivers required to operate the board can be stored in the EEPROMs on the expansion card. This allows integration without manual driver integration or configuration.

Examples of applications with the Raspberry Pi

The Raspberry has almost unlimited uses. These include, for example, the Raspberry Pi as a media center, streaming server, NAS home server or as a particularly inexpensive and compact PC replacement. Other applications are:

- Reader for the CAN bus system in the car,
- Home automation and control of radio sockets,
- PBX,
- router,
- Control of drones,
- own cloud server,
- Game console

Raspberry Pi - what is it actually?

A Raspberry Pi is a fully fledged computer, only in mini format.

A Raspberry Pi is a so-called single-board computer. This means that all the electronic components required for operation - apart from the power supply unit - are housed on a single circuit board.

The mini-computer got its name from the British Raspberry Pi Foundation, which developed it.

Linux distributions such as Raspbian "wheezy" are available as the operating system.

What was the Raspberry Pi developed for?

The Raspberry Pi Foundation set itself the goal of developing a computer that everyone can afford. With the intention that young people would also be able to own a computer with little financial means.

The developers have clearly achieved the goal: You can already purchase a Raspberry Pi for less than 30 euros.

The low price also results from the fact that the Raspberry Pi has no housing. There are no limits to the creativity of the users. You can also use a "classic" housing.

In our special issue manual you will find many possible uses for the Rasperry Pi. For example, you can use it to implement creative projects such as your own robot or home surveillance.

RASPBERRY PI MODELS A AND B

The main component of the Raspberry Pi is a System on Chip (SoC) from Broadcom. It contains a single-core processor with 700 MHz and depending on the model 256 (model A) or 512 MByte (model B) RAM, as well as an OpenGL-ES compatible graphics core, which has a decoder and encoder for MPEG2, MPEG4 and other codecs contains. This makes the Raspberry Pi the perfect and extremely popular DIY media center.

The computing power of the SoC (Broadcom BCM2835) is not particularly large, which is why there are only limited applications for the Raspberry Pi. This in no way limits its skills as an experimental and learning computer. Nevertheless, anyone who experiments with the Raspberry Pi quickly reaches its performance limits. Unfortunately, more powerful alternatives consume more electricity and cost significantly more.

All restrictions can be avoided by clever configuration but it doesn't make it a racehorse. The Raspberry Pi is a handicraft calculator. It is for learning and building close to hardware. That's what it's made for. The fact that a (quite potent) video processor is built in makes it ideal for multimedia applications.

The models A and B differ in that the model B has 512 MB of RAM, an Ethernet port and two USB ports. With only one USB port and 256 MB of RAM, the Model A is more suitable as a control computer that requires low power consumption. Model B is still most suitable for working on a graphical user interface.

Architecture

- System-on-Chip (SoC): BCM2835 ARMv6 from Broadcom
- Processor: 700 MHz single-core CPU
- GPU: VideoCore IV with OpenGL ES 2.0 and OpenVG with hardware acceleration and 1080p30 H.264 high-profile decoding
- RAM: 256 or 512 MB SDRAM

Interfaces

- HDMI 1080p video output (HDMI 1.3 and 1.4)
- Composite video output (PAL/NTSC) via a cinch socket
- Stereo audio output via a 3-pin 3.5mm jack socket
- RJ45 Ethernet connection with 10/100 Mbit/s (model B only)
- 2 x USB 2.0 with a total of 480 MBit/s (only model B)

- 15-pin MPI-CSI connector for HD video camera
- 15-pin serial display interface connector
- 26-pin GPIO header with serial buses
- Micro USB socket for power supply with +5 V/1.2 A
- SD memory card slot

RASPBERRY PI MODELS A + AND B +

The Raspberry Pi Foundation has released improved models with the Raspberry Pi "A +" and "B +". Compared to models A and B, the basic design and the system-on-chip (SoC) have remained the same. So they are not new Raspberry Pis, but rather slightly improved models, in which some defects that have had a negative impact in practice have been eliminated. The improvements have made a decisive contribution to the stability of the hardware. The price of the new models remained within the usual range.

Because the differences between A and A + or B and B + are minimal, the criticism when they were introduced was quite large.

The main features and improvements

More and better USB ports: The USB has 4 ports with improved hot-plugging and energy management (model B +). This is to prevent instabilities when connecting power-hungry devices. The devices can pull together up to 1.2 amperes if it is enabled on the software side and a correspondingly strong power supply unit is available.

Less energy consumption: The use of switching regulators reduced the energy consumption at 5 V from 750 mW to 600 mA. That amounts to 0.5 to 1 W.

More GPIO pins: A total of 40 pins are available while maintaining the previous assignment.

MicroSD: The SD card slot has been replaced by a smaller MicroSD slot. Unfortunately, you can no longer use SD cards. The frequent contact problems are eliminated by changing to microSD cards. MicroSD cards snap into the slot when inserted and can be removed by pressing. In terms of price, there is no great difference between SD cards and MicroSD cards.

Video and audio: The analog video signal no longer comes from a composite video output, but together with the audio signal from a 4-pin 3.5 mm jack socket. The quality of the audio signal has been improved.

Fastening: Two more holes now allow a more convenient fastening.

Dimensions and housing: The dimensions of the board are unchanged. Nevertheless, old housings can no longer be used because the connections have different positions.

LEDs: Two of the three LAN LEDs are located on the RJ45 socket and no longer on the board. The power and activity LEDs (PWR and ACT) are located on the far left under the GPIO connector. The power LED is also used for visual notification of problems with the power supply. If the operating voltage drops below 4.63 volts, this LED begins to flicker and then goes out completely.

Contacts for a button: Below the ACT LED there is an empty RUN header. It has the same function as the P6 of the GPIO interface of the B model. This allows you to connect a button that restarts the Raspberry Pi during operation and after shutting down.

RASPBERRY PI ZERO,
ZERO W AND ZERO WH

The Raspberry Pi Zero is a $5 mini computer. It is basically an improved Raspberry Pi A + with more CPU performance, more RAM and at the same time less power consumption. Usually it is not available individually, but only in a set with a MiniHDMI to HDMI adapter, Micro USB to USB A adapter and a pin header to be soldered yourself. The Zero W differs from the normal Zero in that it has an integrated and combined WLAN and Bluetooth adapter. The Zero WH has a soldered GPIO pin strip.

Raspberry Pi Zero: without WLAN, Bluetooth and soldered GPIO pin strip

Raspberry Pi Zero W: with WLAN and Bluetooth

Raspberry Pi Zero WH: with WLAN and soldered GPIO pin strip

The Raspberry Pi Zero is already clocked at 1,000 MHz by default. Not much more is possible because the old SoC is still installed, which was already installed in the

Raspberry Pi 1. If you need more performance, you should prefer a Raspberry Pi 2 or 3.

In practice, the Raspberry Pi Zero only makes sense if you have little space and can do with the limited connection options, such as the Raspberry Pi A or A +. Otherwise there is a complex and confusing tangle of Raspberry Pi Zero, USB power supply, HDMI and USB adapter cables, USB hub with power supply, WLAN adapter stick, as well as keyboard, mouse and screen.

Architecture

- System-on-chip with BCM2835 from Broadcom
- ARM11 and 1 GHz processor (ARMv6)
- RAM with 512 MB LPDDR2-SDRAM
- Form factor: 65 mm x 30 mm x 5 mm

Interfaces

- Micro SD card slot (pluggable without latching)
- Mini HDMI output with a resolution of 1080p60
- 2 x micro USB connections, one each for power supply and USB
- GPIO header with 40 pins
- Composite video header
- CSI for camera port (Raspberry Pi Zero 1.3 only)

Energy needs

The energy requirement is specified as 0.5 to 0.7 watts and 0.1 to 0.14 amps at 5.09 volts. The idle power consumption is just 0.116 amps.

Raspberry Pi Zero

A single-core BCM2835 SoC from Broadcom is installed, which is clocked at 1 GHz and has a RAM of 512 MB. A slot for a MicroSD card is available as a system drive. The interfaces are a mini HDMI connection for the screen output, an OTG-capable micro USB connection and a micro USB connection for the power supply. Otherwise there are still soldering points for a 40-pin GPIO connector and composite video output.

Version 1.3 of the Raspberry Pi Zero also has the CSI interface for a camera port, as the larger models have.

RASPBERRY PI ZERO W

Just like the Zero (without addition), the Single-Core SoC BCM2835 from Broadcom with 512 MB of RAM is installed in the Zero W, which is also clocked at 1 GHz. The BCM43438 wireless chip for WLAN with 802.11 b/g/n and Bluetooth 4.1 Low-Energy (BLE) is new. This is the same chip as the Raspberry Pi 3 B.

RASPBERRY PI ZERO WH

The equipment of the Raspberry Pi Zero WH corresponds to the Raspberry Pi Zero W. The main difference with the WH model is that the GPIO pin strip is soldered on. This naturally drives up production costs, which is why the Raspberry Pi Zero WH is a little more expensive. You can start right away without having to solder the pin strip.

Initial configuration via SSH for the Raspberry Pi Zero W and WH

As long as WLAN is not set up, the initial configuration via SSH is not possible. There is the following solution:

Enable SSH: There must be an empty file called "ssh" in the boot directory. SSH is permanently activated the first time it boots.

Configure WLAN: There must be a configured wpa_supplicant.conf file in the boot directory. When booting, this is written to the correct directory.

Energy supply: back powering

If you have a stable and clean voltage (low residual ripple) of 5 volts available from a stabilized or regulated power supply, then you can also supply the Raspberry Pi Zero with power via the GPIO 5V pin.

But you should already know what you are doing because the Zero has no poly fuse (fuse) installed. This means that the applied voltage not only supplies the SoC, but also the USB devices. It is possible that not only the SoC breaks, but also the USB devices if you mess up here.

RASPBERRY PI 2 MODEL B

The Raspberry Pi is a mini computer that is very cheap and costs around 40 euros. The "Raspberry Pi 2 Model B" model is a continuous further development of the previous "Raspberry Pi B and B +" models.

The Raspberry Pi 2 contains a quad-core processor from Broadcom, a dual-core GPU and an SDRAM main memory with 1 GB. Compared to its predecessor, the "Raspberry Pi B +", the dimensions of the board (86 x 56 x 20 cm), the position of the interfaces and the wiring of the GPIO pins have remained the same. This means that both housings and extensions can generally continue to be used.

If you are not sure whether you have a "Raspberry Pi B +" or a "Raspberry Pi 2 B", you will find the imprint "Raspberry Pi 2 Model B V1.1" below the GPIO pin header. The processor must also have the Broadcom logo printed on it and the RAM must be on the underside of the board.

The real peculiarity of the Raspberry Pi 2 is not its improved hardware equipment, but the associated possibilities. Thanks to the ARMv7 architecture, more operating systems can be used. For example, Ubuntu and a special version of Windows 10 (from autumn 2015).

Architecture

- System-on-chip: BCM2836 Cortex-A7 ARMv7 from Broadcom
- Processor: Quad-core processor with 900 MHz
- GPU: Dual-core GPU VideoCore IV with OpenGL ES 2.0 and OpenVG with hardware acceleration and 1080p30 H.264 high-profile decoding
- RAM: 1 GB LPDDR2-SDRAM

Interfaces

- HDMI 1080p video output (HDMI 1.3 and 1.4)
- Composite video output (PAL/NTSC) via a 4-pin 3.5mm audio/composite video OUT jack
- Stereo audio output via a 4-pin 3.5mm audio/composite video OUT jack
- RJ45 Ethernet connection with 10/100 Mbit/s
- 4 x USB 2.0 with a total of 480 Mbit/s
- 15-pin MPI-CSI-2 connector for HD video camera
- 15-pin serial display interface connector
- 40-pin GPIO header with serial buses

- Micro USB socket for power supply with +5 V/2 A
- MicroSD memory card slot

Power consumption

As far as energy and electricity consumption is concerned, the Raspberry Pi 2 B hardly differs from the Raspberry Pi B +. The Raspberry Pi 2 only consumes more power under high load.

Performance

An often criticized point is the low computing power of the Raspberry Pi. This has improved a lot with the Raspberry Pi 2. With Pi 2, applications that only employ one core are only a little faster. Only applications that can distribute tasks across multiple cores are up to six times faster.

Due to the change from ARMv6 to ARMv7 you can expect an increase in performance. Simply because the ARMv7 architecture works more effectively. Processes that support multithreading naturally also benefit from all 4 cores. And the additional RAM also has a little positive effect.

How much the performance improves largely depends on what you do. A general statement about the performance cannot be made. You can clearly tell that the Pi 2 is faster than its predecessors.

RASPBERRY PI 3 MODEL B

The Raspberry Pi is a mini computer that is very cheap and only costs around 40 euros. The "Raspberry Pi 3 B" model is a continuous further development of the previous "Raspberry Pi 2 B" model.

The Raspberry Pi 3 contains a quad-core processor with Broadcom's 1.2 GHz and SDRAM RAM with 1 GB.

Compared to its predecessor, the dimensions of the board (86 x 56 x 20 cm), the position of the interfaces and the wiring of the GPIO pins have remained the same. Only the two status LEDs have changed their position, which is why they are no longer visible in one or the other housing.

Instead of the SD card slot with spring mechanism, there is a simple plug-in slot, in which you simply insert and remove the microSD card.

Overall, this means that you can usually continue to use both housings and extensions.

The special features of the Raspberry Pi 3 are that WLAN according to IEEE 802.11 b/g/n and Bluetooth Low

Energy are onboard and do not have to be retrofitted with external USB adapters.

WLAN and Bluetooth onboard

The special feature of the Raspberry Pi 3 is that WLAN according to IEEE 802.11 b/g/n in the 2.4 GHz range with 150 MBit/s and Bluetooth Low Energy are onboard and do not have to be upgraded with external USB adapters.

That means you don't have to buy the necessary components additionally. So it becomes easier to experiment with. You have everything in one and do not have to hope that the additional components purchased will work somehow. In the past there were always problems with hardware detection or driver problems.

Driver problems are excluded because the BCM43143 WLAN chip from Broadcom on the Raspberry Pi 3 B is identical to the official Raspberry Pi WLAN adapter.

In addition, the WLAN chip is not connected to the internal USB, but to the SDIO bus and thus independent of the USB. This should relieve the USB in many applications.

However, the WLAN adapter of the Raspberry Pi 3 only comes to approx. 11 Mbit/s. And yet the effective bandwidth should be higher than with an external WLAN adapter.

Since Raspbian Jessie from 2016-05-10 there is a graphical tool in the task bar of the LXDE desktop environment for managing the internal or an external Bluetooth component. This allows you to select the desired device and establish a Bluetooth connection.

WLAN and Bluetooth onboard also means that you shouldn't touch metal housings, because this severely limits the range of the radio signals. So if you want to use the Raspberry Pi 3 B with WiFi or Bluetooth, then there should already be a plastic housing.

64-bit support

The Raspberry Pi 3 is advertised with its 64-bit support. This is quite normal with modern CPUs today. 64 bit on the hardware side must also be supported by the operating system and software. And this is where the wheat is separated from the chaff. A program must be explicitly designed for 64 bits. However, 64-bit is not used by many programs and depends heavily on the requirements.

In addition, 64 bits can be more of a curse than a blessing. 64 bit also uses twice as much RAM as the same program in 32 bit because the address values are twice as wide and therefore more data has to be transferred.

It is doubtful whether the kernel and the programs will be ported so quickly. Until then, the Raspberry Pi 3 will enjoy at least 40% better performance.

Architecture

- System-on-Chip: BCM2837 64 bit ARMv8 from Broadcom
- Processor: Quad-core processor with 1.2 GHz
- GPU: Dual-core GPU VideoCore IV with OpenGL ES 2.0 and OpenVG with hardware acceleration and 1080p30 H.264 high-profile decoding
- RAM: 1 GB LPDDR2-SDRAM
- WLAN: BCM43143 onboard for IEEE 802.11b, g and n in the 2.4 GHz range
- Bluetooth: Bluetooth Classic and Low Energy (BLE) onboard (Bluetooth 4.1)

The ARMv8 architecture contains Cortex-A53 cores that are faster at the same clock speed than the old Cortex-A7 cores of the Raspberry Pi 2 B. However, only new software benefits from the 64-bit capabilities of the ARMv8 architecture. ARMv8 firmware is only planned for Raspbian later.

However, one can assume that with a little more power consumption, the Raspberry Pi 3 B is about 80 percent faster than the Raspberry Pi 2 B.

Interfaces

- RJ45 Ethernet connection with 10/100 Mbit/s
- 4 x USB 2.0 ports
- 4-pin jack plug with stereo output and composite video
- HDMI port
- 15-pin MPI-CSI-2 connector for HD video camera
- 15-pin serial display interface connector (DSI), e.g. for the official touchscreen display for the Raspberry Pi
- 40-pin GPIO header with serial buses
- MicroSD slot
- Micro USB for connecting a power supply unit with over 2.4 A

RASPBERRY PI 3 MODELS A + AND B +

The Raspberry Pi 3 B + is a slightly improved successor to the Model 3 B. It is characterized by a faster CPU and the long-required Gigabit Ethernet. The unchanged design allows existing housings and plug-on modules to be used further.

The Raspberry Pi 3 A + closes the gap between the Raspberry Pi Zero and the Raspberry Pi 3 B +.

The 3A + model is as fast as a 3B +, but a little cheaper and more economical. The 3A + uses around 1.3 watts less power than the 3B +.

As with the Zero, you have to manage with less RAM, without Ethernet and an integrated USB hub. If you can do without it, the 3A + is an alternative to the slower Raspberry Pi Zero.

- System-on-Chip: BCM2837B0 64 bit ARMv8 from Broadcom
- Processor: Quad-core with Cortex-A53 from 0.6 to 1.4 GHz

- GPU: Dual-core GPU VideoCore IV with OpenGL ES 2.0 and OpenVG with hardware acceleration and 1080p30 H.264 high-profile decoding
- RAM: 1 GB
- Network: LAN7515 for Gigabit Ethernet via USB 2.0
- WLAN: BCM43455 onboard for IEEE 802.11b, g, n and ac in the 2.4 and 5 GHz range
- Bluetooth: Bluetooth Classic and Low Energy (BLE) onboard (Bluetooth 4.2)
- Power-over-Ethernet: Power supply via Ethernet with additional PoE-HAT
- Booting via USB and network (PXE)

Processor

Broadcom's VideoCore IV BCM2837B0 multimedia processor has four ARM cores (Cortex-A53, ARMv8). They work with up to 1.4 GHz. So that the SoC can get rid of its waste heat even at higher clock frequencies, it is equipped with a heat spreader.

Existing software can continue to run without adjustments.

Gigabit Ethernet

The LAN7515 LAN and USB chip is new. There are two USB 2.0 hubs and Gigabit Ethernet. However, the full gigabit data rate cannot be achieved. The data still has to go through the only USB 2.0 port to the VideoCore. With just over 300 Mbit/s, that's the end.

model	Speed (TX)	Speed (RX)
Raspberry Pi 3 B	94.1 Mbit/s	95.5 Mbit/s
Raspberry Pi 3 A +/B +	315 Mbit/s	315 Mbit/s

WiFi for 5 GHz

There is also a new chip for WLAN and Bluetooth (BCM43455). Unlike the predecessor, it also transmits in the 5 GHz band with IEEE 802.11ac on all permissible frequencies. If the Raspberry Pi uses a 5 GHz WLAN, it is much faster.

model	Speed (TX)	Speed (RX)
Raspberry Pi 3 B (2.4 GHz)	35.7 Mbit/s	35.6 Mbit/s
Raspberry Pi 3 A +/B + (2.4 GHz)	46.7 Mbit/s	46.3 Mbit/s
Raspberry Pi 3 A +/B + (5 GHz)	102 Mbit/s	102 Mbit/s

Power supply

Because the Raspberry Pi 3 B + requires more power from scratch, it is important to ensure that a high-quality power supply with at least 2.5 A is used. The official power supply for the Raspberry Pi is recommended.

The new Raspberry Pi can be supplied with power from the Ethernet cable via Power-over-Ethernet (PoE) using four additional pins. An additional plug-on model can draw up to 12.95 watts (according to IEEE 802.af) and thus supply the Raspberry Pi 3 B + with power from a PoE-capable switch

RASPBERRY PI 4 MODEL B

The Raspberry Pi 4 is a powerful mini-computer that has a significant improvement in performance and features compared to its predecessors, while at the same time being backward compatible. The number of possible areas of application has increased significantly. With the Raspberry Pi 4, projects are possible that were previously only possible with limited RAM and interface speeds that were too slow.

The list of features reads like a modern PC:

- CPU: Broadcom BCM2711 with Quad-Core Cortex-A72 (ARM v8), 64 bit, 1.5 GHz
- RAM: 1GB, 2GB or 4GB LPDDR4 SDRAM available
- Video: H.265 (4kp60 decode), H.264 (1080p60 decode, 1080p30 encode), OpenGL ES 1.1, 2.0, 3.0
- WLAN: IEEE 802.11.b/g/n/ac (2.4 and 5 GHz)
- Bluetooth 5.0
- USB: USB 2.0 and 3.0 (2 ports each)
- LAN: Gigabit Ethernet RJ45 port
- GPIO: 40-pin header, HAT compatible

- HDMI: 2 x micro HDMI
- Other: DSI display port, CSI camera port, 4-pin stereo audio and composite video
- Power supply: 5V / 3A via USB-C or GPIO

The Raspberry Pi 4 has new connections and positions of the interfaces. Therefore, the previous housings can only be used with modifications. The front connections are not only interchanged, but are about 1 to 2 mm further forward on the board than on the 3 series.

Comparison

Raspberry Pi 4 BRaspberry Pi 3 B +

main processorARM Cortex-A72 quad-core with 1.5 GHz
ARM Cortex-A53 quad-core with 1.4 GHz

random access memory1, 2 or 4 GB LPDDR4-SDRAM
1 GB LPDDR2-SDRAM

LANGigabit Ethernet

(via USB 3.0 with up to 1,000 Mbit/s)   Gigabit Ethernet

(via USB 2.0 with up to 300 MBit/s)

WIRELESS INTERNET ACCESSIEEE 802.11b/g/n/ac at 2.4 GHz and 5 GHz IEEE 802.11b/g/n/ac at 2.4 GHz and 5 GHz

Bluetooth

Bluetooth 5.0   Bluetooth 4.2

USB2 x USB 2.0/2 x USB 3.0   4 x USB 2.0

multimedia2 x Micro-HDMI (1 x 4k @ 60fps or 2 x 4k @ 30fps) with H.265/H.264   1 x HDMI (1080p @ 60fps) with H.264

power supply5V/3A via USB-C   5V/2.5A via micro USB

Processor and memory

The Raspberry Pi 4 contains a Broadcom processor called BCM2711. This is a quad core with Cortex-A72 (ARM v8) with 64 bits. It is clocked at 1.5 GHz.

The new, powerful processor has been developed for set-top boxes and is accordingly more powerful than the CPUs before, which was developed for smartphones. Of course, electricity consumption also increases.

The Raspberry Pi 4 is available with 1, 2 or 4 GB of RAM, which is LPDDR4-SDRAM. LP stands for low power, i.e. the energy saving variant of SDRAM.

Multimedia

The processor enables 4K content to be played back at a frame rate of 30 frames per second via 2 mini HDMI ports. If only one mini HDMI port is used, the frame rate is up to 60 frames per second.

Streams can be encoded in H.264 and even H.265.

Gigabit Ethernet

Another special feature is the Gigabit Ethernet port with real Gigabit Ethernet speed, which is not limited by an internal USB 2.0 connection.

USB

For USB devices, two USB interfaces with version 2.0 and 3.0 are available.

The USB 3.0 (SuperSpeed) corresponds to USB 3.1 Gen 1 with a speed of 4 GBit/s via both ports together. This corresponds to the equivalent of 500 MByte/s. This is particularly noticeable when connecting external hard drives.

The maximum current that can be drawn from the USB ports is 1.2 amperes in total.

Power supply

Power is supplied via an external USB Type-C power supply with 5 volts/3 amps or 15 watts.

A 2.5-amp power supply can still be used without power-hungry USB devices.

The previously used micro USB power supply can therefore only be used to a limited extent.

Applications

The Raspberry Pi 4 opens up a whole range of new applications:

- Windows 10 on ARM
- Drive-less desktop PC
- Browser based client
- Thin clients
- Raspberry-Pi-Cluster
- NAS with Nextcloud
- Mini Server

RASPBERRY PI: BASICS OF ENERGY SUPPLY/POWER SUPPLY

The power supply of the Raspberry Pi is one of the underestimated sources of error. Mini-computers, like the Raspberry Pi, require a stable voltage AND power supply. With a poor power supply unit and unfavorable operating conditions, strange effects occur in combination with an unstable system behavior.

The effect described in the language Raspberry Pi Forum as "Mysterium" usually manifests itself with terminating LAN and WLAN connections and other malfunctions of devices that are connected to the USB. For example, external WLAN adapters, USB sticks and hard drives.

Problems, nothing but problems!

The effect that occurs is called a "mystery" because, at first glance, the misconduct that occurs has nothing to do with a poor power supply. However, there are an infinite number of problem descriptions in discussion forums. The victims of the mystery report dropouts in the keyboard, mouse, screen display and very often connection problems with LAN and WLAN.

The effects and problems that arise are diverse. Hours of trouble can pass without getting closer to the error. In some serious cases, the error cannot always be reconstructed so easily.

The problems that arise are often related to the fact that the stability of the voltage regulation leaves something to be desired. A lightning symbol in the top right corner of the screen indicates that the danger is imminent.

If the power supply is unsuitable, strange effects can occur during operation.

Why why why?

What does that have to do with the power supply? If you "observe" the power consumption of the Raspberry Pi while using the keyboard, mouse and WLAN adapter with a measuring device, you will notice violent rashes. These USB devices are real power guzzlers. A mouse can draw 50 mA or more current when it is moved. The same applies to a keyboard or a WLAN adapter. These devices are not exactly designed for low power consumption. It is also quite logical. A conventional notebook or PC has an adequately dimensioned power supply. And that should actually be possible with a Raspberry Pi and any other mini-computer. Only the user has to take care of it himself and he takes a conventional plug-in power supply, from his smartphone or another.

Many plug-in power supplies, which are typically used to charge smartphones and tablets, are not power supplies, but usually chargers for battery-operated devices. These chargers rely on the device supplied with them not to expect stable voltage. Battery-powered devices are typically charged with electricity, whereby the stability of the voltage from the charger is completely irrelevant. Only the charging circuit in the device or battery ensures that the battery is charged correctly. This has the advantage that the device manufacturer can install individual batteries and the user can use almost any plug-in power supply.

Not so with a Raspberry Pi or another mini computer. They are dependent on a stabilized operating voltage of approximately 5 volts. If you operate the Raspberry Pi with any power supply, it can and will usually work. However, if the Raspberry Pi and connected USB devices now provide an impulsive current drain, it can happen that the plug-in power supply is overwhelmed, interrupts and the voltage then drops. So falls well below 5 volts.

What happens then? A device that is designed for 5 volts then comes into an unstable operating state. In addition, USB devices expect 5 volts on the USB port. According to the USB specification, a USB device should work between 4.45 and 5.5 volts. There is actually no danger from here.

But now it is the case that the Raspberry Pi also has a say in this. In the event of undervoltage, the Raspberry Pi decommissioned its USB ports in order to restore the stability of the power supply by reducing the current draw. All USB devices go out of operation at least for a short time. And that leads to the malfunctions of individual USB devices or the entire system and explains the dropouts in the USB devices. This applies to the mouse, keyboard, WLAN and LAN connections, as well as USB storage devices.

When the minimum voltage has leveled again, the Raspberry Pi puts the USB and connected devices back into operation. While the keyboard and mouse log in again quickly and automatically, it may be that the LAN and WLAN connections remain deactivated on the software side and have to be activated manually. Unfortunately, in this situation you can no longer access the Raspberry Pi via SSH.

Some users are forced to pull the micro USB connector on the Raspberry Pi and switch it off hard. However, you should avoid this, because "hard switching off" can lead to damage to the file system. If an important system file could not be written to the end at the time of switching off, the hardware, but the file system will not be damaged. In such a case, an incomplete or faulty state can prevent a successful restart. You may also have to complain about data loss.

Plug-in power supplies that are designed as chargers are unsuitable for the energy supply of a Raspberry Pi.

Charger or correct power supply?

Many power supplies that are used on the Raspberry Pi are not real power supplies at all, but rather chargers and therefore only of limited use as "power supplies". But a power supply or power supply differs fundamentally from a charger.

A correct power supply is a voltage source with an electronically limited maximum current. A power supply unit tries to keep the voltage stable up to its maximum current, even with short-term high current draws.

A simple charger is a power source with an electronically limited maximum voltage. The charger simply tries to deliver the maximum current, regardless of the voltage.

This means that a charger is only suitable as a power supply unit if the maximum voltage limit works precisely not only upwards but also downwards. So like a power supply is electronically controlled and does not just consist of a cheap Zener diode.

Unfortunately, now traders and users ignore this. The reason is that both of them don't have the appropriate expertise and don't know the difference between a charger and a real power supply.

The dealers are not entirely innocent. As a rule, they are not experts and cannot judge what they get from the manufacturer or wholesaler and resell to the end customer. For example, the plug-in power supplies advertised as "power supplies" are mostly just simple chargers.

Users in particular suffer from this because they have to rely on the idea that the dealer does not intentionally try to deceive them. Even if the retailer describes or advertises its plug-in power supplies as Raspberry Pi-capable, that means nothing.

Just because 5 volts come out of a black plastic part with a long tail and micro USB connector does not mean that a Raspberry Pi can be operated reliably with it.

GENERAL REQUIREMENTS
FOR ENERGY SUPPLY

Basically, the Raspberry Pi is powered by a voltage of 5.0 volts (V) at the micro USB input. Strictly speaking, it is 5.1 V, which most USB plug-in power supplies also deliver. It is 5.1 V because there are losses due to plug connections and cables. In addition, voltage stabilization is always subject to specimen scatter and minor fluctuations in stabilization. A little overvoltage makes sense at this point.

Of course, you can also operate a Raspberry Pi below 5.0 V. Up to a voltage of 4.75 volts, this shouldn't be a problem. Underneath, you should be very careful to ensure that the operating voltage is stabilized, otherwise considerable instabilities can occur.

Basically, you should not try to operate a Raspberry Pi with undervoltage if you are not familiar with it.

The second important value in energy supply is power consumption, which is given in amperes (A). Exactly how much power the Raspberry Pi needs depends on what is connected to it. As a rule, a power supply with 2 A (2,000 mA) is sufficient. But only if you don't connect power-hungry USB devices. Then you need an externally powered USB hub or you should use a power supply with at least 2.5 A (2,500 mA). It is important to know that a Raspberry Pi cannot draw more than 2.5 A. If the entire system needs more electricity, this is limited by a fuse and can lead to instabilities.

The voltage (volt, V) of a power supply is a nominal value that must be observed. This means that the power supply voltage and the device operating voltage must match. The two values must not differ significantly from one another.

The current (ampere, A) and the power (watt, W) of a power supply, on the other hand, are nominal values that must not be exceeded. It should be noted here that a 10 W or 2 A power supply unit (at 5 V) must not be operated at the nominal value or beyond. If you want to pull the 2 A, the power supply is inevitably brought into an unstable state. That means the voltage breaks down and the supplied device fails. If you need 2 A, you never use a 2 A power supply, but one step above it. At least 20% to 30% more. So at least 2.5 A. Better more.

USB

In general, every USB device without its own power supply must be powered by the Raspberry Pi. The current draw can vary greatly depending on the device. For example, the current consumption of a keyboard, just as an example, can be between 0.1 A and 0.5 A (100 mA and 500 mA). To make matters worse, USB devices can draw impulses quite impulsively. That can get the Raspberry Pi or the power supply out of step.

For safe continuous operation, the power consumption of the USB devices must be checked individually. If you notice instabilities on the part of the Raspberry Pi, then an externally powered USB hub is a solution. It is better to use USB devices that do not consume as much power.

GPIO

What does the GPIO have to do with the energy supply of a Raspberry Pi? If you connect the GPIO header, then quite a bit.

A single GPIO port can deliver a maximum of 16 mA without being damaged. All GPIO pins together a maximum of 50 mA. Assuming 40 pins, of which only 26 pieces can be connected as GPIO, the current that you can draw from a GPIO port if you use them all as an output is just 2 mA.

Since not all pins will be used as an output at the same time, the current draw per pin should not be higher than 3 to 5 mA. The fewer, the more pins you can use as an output and the more stable the Raspberry Pi runs.

HDMI

What does the HDMI have to do with the power supply of a Raspberry Pi? If you want to connect a screen to the HDMI port, then a lot. On average, the HDMI connection consumes up to 50 mA of current (measured).

From the Raspberry Pi B + onwards, up to 400 mA can be drawn. This is important for HDMI devices without their own power supply. HDMI to VGA converters get enough power from the HDMI port.

Ethernet port (RJ45)

What does the Ethernet port have to do with the power supply of a Raspberry Pi? Again, if you want to connect the Raspberry Pi to the network via it, then quite a bit.

If you have connected a remote station to the Ethernet port with a cable, the current draw is around 60 mA (measured).

CSI - Camera Connector Interface

A camera module for the Camera Connector (CSI) requires around 0.25 A (250 mA). Unfortunately, it was not possible to find out whether this was true, because the data sheets of the relevant providers do not provide any information about the power consumption of your camera modules.

Summary: Power Consumption (Official)
Raspberry Pipower consumption
Board (typical)USB peripheralsMaximum
Model A200 mA   500 mA 700 mA
Model B500 mA500 mA 1.2 A
Model A +180 mA   500 mA 700 mA
Model B +330 mA   600 mA/1.2 A (can be activated)   1.8 A
Model 2 B330 mA   600 mA/1.2 A (can be activated)   1.8 A
Model 3 B330 mA   600 mA/1.2 A (can be activated)   1.8 A

POWER SUPPLY: RASPBERRY PI
MODEL A AND B

The requirements of the Raspberry Pi model A and B are 5 V and 0.7 A (700 mA), which corresponds to 3.5 W. The Raspberry Pi only reaches 0.7 A if you also operate an HDMI monitor, Ethernet network and USB devices. In addition, there is the power consumption of these devices when they are powered by the Raspberry Pi.

- Raspberry Pi: approx. 700 mA
- HDMI: approx. 50 mA
- Ethernet: approx. 50 mA
- USB: approx. 200 mA

Total power consumption makes up 1 A (1,000 mA), protected by a fuse. A 1.2 A power supply is recommended. The reason is that a power supply should never be operated too close to its nominal load. So if you calculate with 1 A, you take 10 to 20% more. This is the only way to ensure that the power supply is stable. If even more current is drawn for a short time than the power supply can deliver, then the voltage drops, which acts like switching off the voltage and the Raspberry Pi runs out.

If you do not fully exploit the Raspberry Pi with all its possibilities, you can get by with a power supply of 1.0 A or less. But only in exceptional cases.

There are often reports that the Raspberry Pi Model B does not run very stably and occasionally gets out and then has to be restarted. The reason: The power supply of the model B is a bit shaky, which is why a real power supply, no charger, with at least 1.2 A and more is recommended. If you use a power supply with less than 1.2 A, you have to expect instabilities. Especially if you still operate devices on HDMI and USB that do not have their own power supply and therefore pull out of the interface.

In case of doubt, the operation of USB devices on an externally powered USB hub is always recommended.

Power supply: Raspberry Pi model B +

A major advantage of the B + model is the better stability of the power supply overall. Not only can 4 USB devices be connected to the B + model, but also without an externally powered USB hub.

Overall, the B + 2.0 A (2,000 mA) can draw from its power supply. Provided that the power supply delivers that too.

- Raspberry Pi: approx. 500 mA
- HDMI: approx. 50 mA
- Ethernet: approx. 50 mA
- USB: approx.1,400 mA

The current consumption of the B + is given as 0.6 A (600 mA). If you work with a monitor, keyboard, mouse and Ethernet, this corresponds to measurable values. So it needs less than Model B and should run more stable overall with the same power supply.

According to the specification, all USB 2.0 ports of the B + together provide 0.6 A (600 mA). That should be enough for a 2.5-inch USB hard drive. But not always. Overall, about 1.5 A (1,500 mA) remain for the USB devices. Unless you also use HDMI and Ethernet. Then it's a little less. But surely enough for most USB devices.

To be able to draw the maximum of 1.2 A (1,200 mA) from a USB port, you have to do this in the file "/boot/config.txt" with the line "safe_mode_gpio = 4" (old firmware) or " Unlock max_usb_current = 1 "(new firmware) to remove the maximum current draw of 600 mA. There is this limit so that the Raspberry Pi does not become unstable and goes out when it is power-hungry.

Power supply: Raspberry Pi 2 B

A 5.1 V and 2.5 A power supply is recommended for the Raspberry Pi 2 B. It is certainly possible under 2.0 A. But if you want to operate other devices on the USB ports besides the mouse and keyboard, then you should use a power supply unit with high current if you want to ensure a stable power supply.

Power supply: Raspberry Pi 3 B

Especially with the Raspberry Pi 3 you should know that it has a design flaw. Due to a new printed circuit board design and savings in the use of inferior components, the path between the micro USB socket and the chip drops by up to 0.6 volts. As a result, the Raspberry Pi 3 is operated with a conventional USB power supply with 5.1 V at the undervoltage limit. The problem is solved by the fact that the official power supply for the Raspberry Pi 3 has a voltage of 5.2 volts.

Note: Due to component and production tolerances, not every Raspberry Pi 3 is affected.

Power supply: Raspberry Pi 4 B

In contrast to the models before, the Raspberry Pi 4 B needs a USB power supply with 5 volts and 3 amps with USB Type-C (plug connection).

It should be noted that the Raspberry Pi 4 B has an incorrectly implemented USB-C port and active USB-C cables (with an E-Mark chip) recognize the Raspberry Pi 4 B as an audio adapter and therefore do not output any current,

A simple USB-C cable without the E-Mark chip can help. Such cables are usually included as charging cables for smartphones. The usual cables for notebooks, Thunderbold etc. are not suitable for operating the Raspberry Pi 4 B.

The Raspberry Pi Foundation has announced a revision, which is why there will be newer Raspberry Pi 4 B that do not have this problem.

Power supply: troubleshooting

A flashing red LED on the Raspberry Pi indicates a problem with the power supply. You should take care of it urgently, because then the operation of the Raspberry Pi can no longer be ensured and functional failures can occur. As a rule, the problem can be found in connection with power-hungry USB devices or a low-power power supply.

Back-Powering

The Raspberry Pi (1) Model A and Model B have a nice feature. The entire power supply and the USB ports are connected to one line. Back-powering can be carried out via the USB interface.

One only has to take care that all protective mechanisms are bypassed. There are also indications that data loss can occur on the SD card.

In particular, the operation of active USB hubs on models A and B can unintentionally lead to back powering, because here the hub feeds the Raspberry Pi through the USB port, although the Raspberry Pi is already supplied with a USB power supply.

The risks of unwanted back-powering should not be underestimated. In principle, only a USB hub that has been specially designed for operation on a Raspberry Pi can help here.

The right power supply

To avoid the various problems with an unstable power supply, you should use a "real" power supply with a stabilized voltage. Buying power supplies for the Raspberry Pi is therefore always a game of chance. To avoid a bad buy, you should only buy power supplies where they are explicitly available as accessories for the Raspberry Pi.

RASPBERRY PI: FIRST STEPS IN CONFIGURATION (Basic configuration)

After starting up the Raspberry Pi for the first time, you should carry out a basic configuration before you start working on possible installations and configurations.

This includes the configuration of language, character set, time zone and a German keyboard layout. In addition, you should also change the default password of the user "pi" and update the system software. After that, the basic configuration of the Raspberry Pi is already done.

For the configuration of Raspbian there is a configuration tool under "Preferences> Raspberry Pi Configuration". This allows you to quickly configure the important things without having to enter complicated commands on the command line.

With some changes you will be asked if you want to restart the system. Basically, you can first make all changes and then restart.

Basic configuration with the command line and via SSH

For basic configuration, Raspbian comes with the command line tool "Raspberry Pi Software Configuration Tool", with which the important things can be configured quickly without having to enter complicated commands on the command line.

Basic configuration: step by step

Depending on the application and requirement, additional or different configuration steps may result.

1. Change language
2. Change keyboard layout
3. Change time zone
4. Change the WLAN country code
5. Change default password
6. Change hostname (optional)
7. Activate SSH and create new SSH key (optional)
8. Set screen resolution (optional)
9. Extend file system (optional)
10. Update software
11. Change the name of the network interfaces

Note: Almost all configuration changes only take effect after a restart. However, you can make almost all changes at the same time and then apply all changes together with a restart.

1. Change language

Those who speak English can ignore this. As a rule, however, the display and presentation in the German language is preferred.

Menu order in German: Settings/Raspberry Pi configuration/Localization/Specify speaking environment

Menu order in English: Preferences/Raspberry Pi Configuration/Localization/Set Locale

Here you select the following values in the fields:

- Language: de (German)
- Country (Country): DE (Germany)
- Character set: UTF-8

Apply the setting with "OK". You can then make further settings or exit the configuration tool by clicking "OK". If so, restart to start the system with the changed settings.

2. Change the keyboard layout

As a rule, all images that have an English language setting also have an English keyboard layout. This setting is about setting the keyboard layout as the keys are printed. By default, an English assignment is set, for example, where Y and Z are interchanged. With a

German keyboard you would have to press the Z for a Y. To avoid this and further confusion, it is recommended to select the correct keyboard layout.

Menu order in German: Settings/Raspberry Pi configuration/Localization/Define keyboard

Menu order in English: Preferences/Raspberry Pi Configuration/Localization/Set Keyboard

Here you select the following values in the fields:

- Country (Country): Germany/Deutschland
- Variant: German/Deutsch

There are various options for the keyboard variant. You should choose the variant that probably fits the keyboard.

3. Change time zone

The time zone is used to determine the correct time at a specific location. The default setting is usually incorrect. Therefore you have to choose the time zone in which you are located and whose time you want to be displayed correctly.

Menu order in German: Settings/Raspberry Pi configuration/Localization/Time zone

Menu order in English: Preferences/Raspberry Pi Configuration/Localization/Set Timezone

Here you select the following values in the fields:

- Area: Europe
- Location: Berlin

4. Change the WLAN country code

The WLAN country code is used to select a type of profile for using the frequency spectrum in which WLANs are operated. Almost every country has set a different operating license for this, which is set in a country profile.

Menu order in German: Settings/Raspberry Pi configuration/Localization/WiFi country

Menu order in English: Preferences/Raspberry Pi Configuration/Localization/Set Wifi Country

Here you select the following values in the fields:

- Country (Country): DE Germany

Note: If the country code remains at the standard value "GB", it may be that the integrated and external WLAN adapter does not recognize WLANs in Germany.

5. Change the default password

Every standard installation knows standard users with standard passwords. After commissioning, these standard passwords must be changed. With the Raspberry Pi with Raspbian this only affects the user "pi". If you are running a Raspberry Pi in the network, the first official action, after changing the language and country settings, should be changing the password.

Menu order in German: Settings/Raspberry Pi configuration/System/Change password

Menu order in English: Preferences/Raspberry Pi Configuration/System/Change Password

Note: After the first start-up of a Raspberry Pi, it is generally recommended to change the default password of the user "pi". If you leave it on "raspberry", strangers can also access the Raspberry Pi. Both locally via screen and keyboard, as well as via SSH over the network.

6. Change hostname (optional)

The host name defines the computer name under which the Raspberry Pi can be reached in the network. By default, a fresh Raspbian has the host name "raspberrypi". You might want to change that. For example, if you run several, then you might want to differentiate them by name.

Menu order in German: Settings/Raspberry Pi configuration/System/Hostname/OK

Menu order in English: Preferences/Raspberry Pi Configuration/System/Hostname/OK

The new host name can be entered in the text field with the given name. It is saved with a click on "OK", but only accepted when you restart.

If you want to do it manually:

- sudo hostname -b {NEW_NAME}
- Then check briefly:
- hostname

Note: It is advisable to change the host name using the Raspberry Pi configuration tool.

It is important that if you have changed the hostname, you also have to re-create the SSH keys.

7. Activate SSH and recreate SSH key (optional)

Distribution images contain a key for the SSH server, with which the Raspberry Pi authenticates itself to the client. If you have drawn a corresponding image onto your SD memory card, then this key is the same everywhere. However, a key should be unique, otherwise it is not suitable for secure authentication. Therefore, you should change this key during an initial configuration.

First we delete all files in which the keys are located. There are several of them.

sudo rm / etc / ssh / ssh_host_ *

We then reconfigure the SSH server. The key files are created automatically.

sudo dpkg-reconfigure openssh-server

With a new Raspbian image, SSH is deactivated or switched off by default. It can be activated via "raspi-config" or activated and started on the command line.

Start (activate) SSH automatically:

- sudo systemctl enable ssh
- Start SSH:
- sudo systemctl start ssh

After logging in again via SSH, you will have to re-confirm the identity of the Raspberry Pi.

8. Set screen resolution (optional)

Usually Raspbian sets the appropriate resolution itself. Sometimes it can make sense to change them.

sudo raspi-config

Here you can find the resolution setting in "Advanced Options/Resolution".

9. Extend file system (optional)

If a Linux distribution was freshly written on an SD card, the root partition does not occupy the entire memory card, but leaves a part of it unused.

When you start a newly flashed Raspbian Jessie (from 2016-05-10), the file system is automatically expanded to the total size of the memory card. Therefore, it is usually not necessary to expand the file system.

Menu order in German: Settings/Raspberry Pi configuration/System/File system expand

Menu order in English: Preferences/Raspberry Pi Configuration/System/Expand Filesystem

After that, a restart is mandatory.

10. Update software

Especially when commissioning and basic configuration for the first time, it is important that the system is updated on the software side. Updating all installed applications and libraries of a Raspbian after the first start-up consists of two steps.

- sudo apt-get update
- sudo apt-get dist-upgrade

Depending on the application and requirement, you should be careful with subsequent updates. With the update, you can also shoot a system with its configuration.

11. Change the name of the network interfaces

Since Raspbian Stretch, the network interfaces for Ethernet and WLAN have had different names. So no longer "eth0" and "wlan0", but "enx..." and "wlx...". This applies to network adapters connected via USB, which deviate from the usual names. This means that when configuring the network, you first have to determine the individual name or change the name to the old method.

Important: restart Raspberry Pi

After making extensive changes to the configuration, you should always restart the Raspberry Pi.

sudo reboot

Only when the system has accepted the changes and then runs smoothly can the system be used for experiments and further configuration.

Extension: network configuration

If you want to access a Raspberry Pi more often via SSH, a static IP configuration is recommended. You set up a fixed IPv4 address that no longer changes on its own.

Raspberry Pi: measure power consumption

There are many different statements and statements regarding the power consumption of the Raspberry Pi. Some have actually measured electricity consumption. And now these values are haunting around in forums and blogs. Unfortunately, these measurements are of little help if it is not known how and what was measured. Both the measurement and the measurement result must then be viewed critically. Such a measurement result is usually worthless if nothing is known about how the measurement result came about. To make matters worse, each measurement result must always be interpreted correctly.

Measurement setup

Every measurement requires a defined measurement setup. This is the only way to ensure that a measurement delivers the same values again at a later point in time. Once the measurement setup has been documented, the measured values can still be traced later without having to repeat the measurement.

Raspberry Pi model A, A +, B (Rev. 2), B +, RPi 2 B, RPi Zero and as comparison an Odroid-C1
Power supply: USB power supply with 5 V/2.1 A
SD card: Noname microSDHC/Class 10/8 GB
Screen: HDMI monitor
WLAN adapter 1: Noname USB 2.0 Wireless/IEEE 802.11n/chipset Ralink 5370
WLAN adapter 2: Noname USB 2.0 Wireless/IEEE 802.11n/chipset Ralink 5372
Keyboard: Hama Slim Line SL 640 (5V/0.5A max.)
Mouse: Noname Optical Wheel Mouse (5V/50mA)

This measurement setup provides that the measurement takes place behind the power supply unit that supplies the Raspberry Pi with power. The reason is that the power supply has its own consumption, which depends on the power supply and current draw and falsifies the measured values. The pure power consumption of the Raspberry Pi with any connected components is interesting.

In order to avoid a measurement error due to different memory cards, a microSDHC card was used as the storage medium for all measurements. This is necessary because the Raspberry Pi B + does not accept normal SD cards. The microSDHC card with an SD card adapter was therefore used in the A and B models.

Measuring device: USB Power Meter from PortaPow

The measuring device is a PortaPow Premium USB + DC Power Monitor. This allows you to measure voltage, current and power at the same time on a USB port. To do this, the Power Monitor is looped into the power supply of the Raspberry Pi. For this purpose the Power Monitor has a USB-A plug and a USB-A socket. The measuring device has its own power supply and does not load the USB power supply.

Data logging

Voltage, current and power were measured. The current was measured twice. Once during the boot process. The current value was continuously observed as it fluctuated. The highest value was recorded (current peak).

The second measurement of the current was made after the boot process was completed, the login was displayed and the Raspberry Pi was not yet used. So when logged out and without additional active software or users. In this case, the measuring device displayed the measured values without fluctuation.

The tension was usually between 5.11 and 5.16 V. The higher the current draw, the more the voltage is pressed. However, the value is no longer exciting, unless you want to calculate the performance.

The performance is arithmetically a product of voltage and current. It is also displayed by the measuring device. Unfortunately, the calculation is not entirely correct, which is certainly due to the tolerance. With the second and third digits after the decimal point, this is not so tragic. This inaccuracy is just about acceptable.

Measurement 1: Raspberry Pi naked

During this measurement, the Raspberry Pi was operated without any other connected devices.

model	tension	electricity	power	Current (peak)
RPi A	5.157 V	0.116 A	0.603 W.	0.198 A.
RPi A +	5.160 V	0.085 A.	0.438 W.	0.150 A

	Voltage	Current	Power	
RPi Zero	5.166 V	0.084 A.	0.433 W.	0.170 A.
RPi B	5.139 V	0.341 A.	1.752 W.	0.422 A.
RPi B +	5.150 V	0.203 A.	1.045 W.	0.264 A.
RPi 2 B	5.151 V	0.199 A.	1.025 W.	0.345 A.
ODROID-C1	5.152 V	0.192 A.	0.989 W.	0.443 A.

In the basic state, the B + model consumes around 140 mA or 700 mW less than the B model. The Raspberry P 2 B does not differ significantly from the B + model. The Raspberry Pi Zero and A + models are the most economical.

Measurement 2: Rasperry Pi with Ethernet

During this measurement, the Raspberry Pi was connected to the local network via Ethernet. This is known as headless mode, in which the Raspberry Pi is operated without a screen and keyboard. An SSH connection can be established over the network and the Raspberry Pi can be operated remotely. During this measurement, the SSH connection was only briefly tested for accessibility.

model	tension	electricity	power	Current (peak)
RPi A	no ethernet port			
RPi A +	no ethernet port			
RPi Zero	no ethernet port			
RPi B	5.134 V	0.400 A.	2.053 W.	0.483 A.
RPi B +	5.146 V	0.242 A.	1.245 W.	0.308 A.
RPi 2 B	5.147 V	0.237 A.	1.224 W.	0.424 A.
ODROID-C1	5.146 V	0.225 A.	1.148 W.	0.485 A.

The power consumption of the Ethernet port is 20 mA lower for the B + model than for the B model. Because there is no Ethernet port on models A, A + and Zero, this measurement makes no sense on these models.

Measurement 3: Raspberry Pi with WLAN adapter

In this measurement, the Raspberry Pi was operated with a WLAN adapter in headless mode. A connection to the WLAN was not configured.

Two different WLAN adapters for the USB are available for this measurement. The first is a nano-type one. The second is larger and has an external antenna.

model	tension	electricity	power	Current (peak)
RPi A	5.148 V	0.221 A.	1.143 W.	0.300 A.
RPi A +	5.151 V	0.185 A.	0.958 W.	0.247 A.
RPi Zero	5.129 V	0.179 A.	0.918 W.	0.263 A.
RPi B	5.131 V	0.445 A.	2.277 W.	0.510 A.
RPi B +	5.141 V	0.300 A.	1.537 W.	0.354 A.
RPi 2 B	5.143 V	0.294 A.	1.512 W.	0.406 A.
ODROID-C1	5.141 V	0.288 A.	1.486 W	0.526 A.

model	tension	electricity	power	Current (peak)
RPi A	5.143 V	0.295 A.	1.522 W.	0.357 A.
RPi A +	5.146 V	0.254 A.	1.312 W.	0.307 A.
RPI Zero	5.127 V	0.241 A.	1.245 W.	0.318 A.
RPi B	5.125 V	0.515 A.	2.639 W.	0.571 A.

RPi B +5.137 V   0.368 A.   1.890 W.   0.509 A.

RPi 2 B5.137 V   0.368 A.   1.890 W.   0.463 A.

ODROID-C15.137 V   0.353 A.   1.818   W.   0.606 A.

The second WLAN adapter consumes around 60 to 70 mA more electricity.

Measurement 4: Raspberry Pi with monitor and keyboard (normal operation 1)

For this measurement, the Raspberry Pi was operated with an HDMI monitor and keyboard. The connection to the local network via Ethernet or WLAN was not intended for this measurement.

modeltensionelectricitypowerCurrent (peak)

RPi A5.146 V   0.239 A.   1.229 W.   0.312 A.

RPi A +5.150 V   0.204 A 1.050 W.   0.271 A.

RPI Zero5.129 V0.089 A.   0.451 W.   0.204 A.

RPi B5.126 V   0.465 A.   2.384 W.   0.553 A.

RPi B +5.136 V   0.329 A.   1,689 W.   0.391 A.

RPi 2 B5.141 V 0.321 A.   1.650 W.   0.508 A.

ODROID-C15.138 V   0.368 A.   1.891   W. 0.604 A.

Here, the effect of the Raspberry Pi Zero was that not using the keyboard did not result in any power consumption. When using the keyboard, the power consumption increased by around 20 mA.

Measurement 5: Raspberry Pi with monitor, keyboard, mouse and Ethernet (normal operation 2)

For this measurement, the Raspberry Pi was operated with a VGA monitor, keyboard and mouse. An HDMI to VGA adapter was utilized to use the monitor. The connection to the local network was made via Ethernet.

modeltensionelectricitypowerCurrent (peak)

RPi A only one USB port and no Ethernet port
RPi A +only one USB port and no Ethernet port
RPi Zero only one USB port and no Ethernet port
RPi B5.120 V   0.590 A.   3.090 W.   0.649 A.

RPi B +5.134 V 0.431 A.   2.211 W.   0.460 A.

RPi 2 B5.131 V 0.426 A.   2.085 W.   0.571 A.

ODROID-C15.122 V   0.552 A.   2.827   W.
         0.748 A.

Note: In this case, the current was measured while the mouse was moving. When the mouse is at rest, the power consumption has decreased by approx. 32 mA.

Measurement 6: Raspberry Pi with approx. 1% CPU utilization

For this measurement, the Raspberry Pi was operated with a VGA monitor, keyboard and mouse. An HDMI to VGA adapter was used to use the monitor. The connection to the local network was made via Ethernet.

During the recording of the measured values, it was ensured that "top" showed almost 1% CPU utilization.

modeltensionelectricityPower (measured)

RPi B5.121 V   0.558 A.   2,857 W
RPi B +5.134 V   0.401 A.   2.053 W.
RPi 2 B5.133 V   0.393 A.   2.058 W.

Measurement 7: Raspberry Pi with approx. 100% CPU utilization

For this measurement, the Raspberry Pi was operated with a VGA monitor, keyboard and mouse. An HDMI to

VGA adapter was used to use the monitor. The connection to the local network was made via Ethernet.

During the recording of the measured values, it was ensured that "top" displayed almost 100% CPU utilization. The CPU usage was triggered with "sudo apt-get update" and "sudo apt-get upgrade".

model tension electricity Performance (calculated)

RPi B	5.119 V	0.648 A.	3.317 W.
RPi B +	5.136 V	0.494 A.	2.537 W.

RPi 2 B coming soon

The difference in power consumption between approx. 1% CPU utilization (measurement 6) and approx. 100% CPU utilization (measurement 7) is approx. 90 to 100 mA. At approx. 5 V USB voltage, this is approx. 500 mW.

Summary of knowledge

The Raspberry Pi Zero uses the least electricity. It has the least connections for this.

The B + model consumes between 100 and 150 mA less current than the B model. That amounts to between 500 and 700 mW.

The difference in power consumption between approx. 1% and approx. 100% CPU utilization is approx. 90 to 100 mA. Both the B + and B models.

The differences between RPi B + and RPi 2 B are found in the second digit after the decimal point.

The power consumption also varies with the use of the periphery. The mouse or keyboard that is used consume more power than the mouse and keyboard that are at rest.

RASPBERRY PI PROJECTS - THE TOP 10

It should be clear to everyone by now that the Raspberry Pi can be used to implement some cool projects with little effort. The single-board computer is not only suitable for programming professionals, but also offers exciting opportunities for beginners. In the following we want to take a look at the most impressive Raspberry Pi projects of recent times.

Raspberry Pi projects: Game Boy

Two cult objects meet here: The 27-year-old Game Boy and the only four-year-old Raspberry Pi. To bring the two together, you can either go to work martially and cannibalize the Game Boy, use a Raspberry Pi and then the RetroPie operating system to install. If you don't want to be so brutal, you have two other options: cheap replicas or 3D printing.

The former is based on the ZeroBOY project; here, a Raspberry Pi Zero is used, which is integrated into a Game Boy case. The necessary parts such as PCB controller board, tactile buttons and monitor are connected via the GPIO pins of the Zeros. In addition to detailed instructions with a list of all components, the project website also has an "all-in-one" distribution that can be easily installed on the mini computer via microSD.

The other variant is the 3D-printed Game Boy, which is joined by a Raspberry Pi, a TFT touchscreen display and an old SNES controller as a parts supplier. A finished emulator program is available as software that can be installed directly on the Raspi.

Raspberry Pi projects: 3D printed drone

The Raspberry Pi learns to fly! The Open DIY Projects cooperation has developed an entry-level copter that dispenses with complex accessories, but still relies on high-tech. The WiFree Copter is controlled with a smartphone and transmits the digital HD image live on the display. The flight electronics are controlled by a Raspberry Pi, which is connected to the smartphone via WiFi. In addition, a Raspberry Pi camera module transmits video recordings in real time. The housing of the copter is printed in a 3D printer; the whole project is open source.

Raspberry Pi projects: Wizard chess à la Harry Potter

Do you remember Harry Potter and the Philosopher's Stone? In order to get to this, a round of magician chess must be completed in addition to other difficult tasks. To do this, you have to maneuver victoriously through the game as one of the animated chess pieces, in which one or the other time heads roll. The version of Bethanie Fentiman is not that martial, but the project is quite impressive. The chess system consists of stepper motors, slide rails, gear wheels, magnets and much more. In addition, Bethanie has written all sorts of chess moves in the program.

Raspberry Pi projects: parallel computing

The view of the almost three meter high sculpture supercomputer combo is quite impressive. Each of the 256 Raspberry Pi Model B + s is connected to a plastic panel and the corresponding freely movable arm swings outwards as soon as a Pi is actively working on a parallel computing task. When the mini-computers are activated, you feel a bit like in a science fiction film: the green, translucent panels slide in hypnotic waves over the spiral surface to provide a physical representation of the calculations performed.

17 PROJECTS TO BE IMPLEMENTED WITH THE RASPBERRY PI

At first glance the Raspberry Pi does not appear to be anything special: it is simply a computer card with different components, almost the same size as a credit card, and for this reason, it is surprising how many possibilities this small computer offers.

Developed by an organization in Great Britain, the Raspberry Pi Foundation, the mini computer is offered at extremely advantageous prices and is now the best-selling English computer of all time. Originally it was designed for young technology enthusiasts, but due to the minimal technical equipment and the absence of the case, the Raspberry Pi is particularly suitable for learning about the hardware structures of a computer and starting to try one's hand at programming.

In a short time, the mini computer has awakened the interest of clever and do-it-yourself users, who have been able to realize ideas of different nature thanks to the Raspberry Pi. Thus were born countless original projects and applications for the Raspberry Pi.

What can you do with a web server on the Raspberry Pi?

If you use a Raspberry Pi as a web server, you should know that it has limited hardware. Computer performance is lower than a common web server, which is provided by a provider. The Raspberry Pi is not very suitable for managing complex sites (such as online shops or sites with dynamic content) or for those with a high number of visitors. Often even the low bandwidth of your Internet connection is an impediment to the use of a Raspberry Pi as a complete server.

However, there are different fields of application for a web server, managed on a Raspberry Pi, for example, you can use it as a home server with Internet access or use it in a corporate network. On this, you can test the web pages before putting them online or completely manage small sites with few visitors on your own. You can also create your own Cloud and configure home automation programs (lights, radiators, etc.).

Another advantage is the low running costs of a web server on the Raspberry Pi, as it requires only an Internet connection and the current, which generally uses just over 5 watts. Even if a web server is constantly running, consumption will not affect your bill much.

Furthermore, the one-off costs of configuring the necessary components are also easily predictable.

The requirements to set up a web server on the Raspberry Pi

The web server presented here is only one of many variants for using a Raspberry Pi as a web server. Besides the mini-computer they are also necessary:

- an SD card on which to set the Raspbian operating system;
- an Internet connection, via network cable (recommended) or Wi-Fi;
- the current for the micro USB cable.

The most energy-saving variant is obtained with a "headless" web server, i.e. without a screen and input devices, which should be configured with remote access to the server via SSH: thanks to an SSH client (such as PuTTY and WinSCP) for Windows or OpenSSH for UNIX operating systems) you can set up a web server using a computer, a smartphone or other devices and make the necessary changes. If you have decided to administer the server via SSH, enter the IPv4 address of your Raspberry Pi in the client to make the connection. If you don't know the IP address of your Raspberry Pi, you can find out by entering the command hostname −I in the terminal (or alternatively config). If, on the other hand, you use the Raspberry Pi headless, find the address to enter on your router, opening the router's settings page on your browser (usually located at 192.168.0.1 or on fritz.box, if you have a Fritz! Box).

If you want to use the webserver to build a private cloud or other applications that need more space, you should expand the memory capacity. This operation is easily possible using a pen drive or an external hard drive.

Make a server reachable always at the same IP address

Not only must the servers always be online, so that users can access them at any time, but they must also be reachable at the same IP address. Generally, a home server has a dynamic IP address, which then changes regularly (usually every 24 hours) and prevents the server from being reachable at the same IP address. For this, it would be better to use a static IP address, but not all providers offer it (and if so, only upon payment of an additional monthly cost).

There are also other possibilities to manage a server at the same address, that is through dynamic DNS (DDNS). There are both paid and free DDNS services. Here you register a domain name and connect it with a computer or router. A software always automatically assigns a domain name to the current IP address of your Internet connection, so that the server remains continuously accessible online with the same name.

You also have another option available, if you use a Fritz! Box router and connect to the Internet via this: find more information on how to configure dynamic DNS on your router on the manufacturer's page.

Set up a web server with LAMP on the Raspberry Pi

Thanks to this tutorial, configure the LAMP platform on a web server of your Raspberry Pi. LAMP is the acronym for a software package, composed of the following parts: a Linux operating system (in this tutorial we will use the one already pre-installed on the device, Raspbian), an Apache web server, a MySQL database and the PHP scripting language. In addition to the LAMP package, the phpMyAdmin database program is also installed.

First, log in to the console (terminal) of your Raspberry Pi. Before starting with the configuration of the LAMP package, you should update all the packages already installed with these commands:

- sudo apt-get update
- sudo apt-get upgrade

Now you can start configuring the individual LAMP components. In the tutorial, we will guide you through the various steps to highlight the intermediate steps and to explain them better. So some important reports will be explained, and some tests will be shown with which you can verify the operation of the installation.

Set Apache

The installation of an Apache HTTP server occurs quickly. A single command is enough to configure it, and the same is true for the other three components of the LAMP suite for the Raspberry Pi web server. To install Apache 2, enter the following command in the terminal:

- sudo apt-get install apache2

To check if the installation was successful, enter the IP address of the Raspberry Pi in the address bar of your browser. If Apache 2 has been configured correctly, a preset page with the word "It works" appears in the browser. This HTML page is found in Raspbian Jessie in the /var/www/html/index.html folder, while in the old version of Raspbian (Wheezy) it is instead created in the /var/www/index.html directory. In the folder you can edit and create all the pages you want:

sudo nano /var/www/index.html

or

sudo nano /var/www/html/index.html

Once you've made the changes, you should be able to see them after updating the page in the browser.

Set up PHP

Now install PHP 5, so that the webserver can also process PHP scripts and not just HTML, CSS and JavaScript files:

sudo apt-get install php5 libapache2-mod-php5

You can generate a PHP file in the / var / www directory. To make a test create the file phpinfo.php:

sudo nano phpinfo.php

Use an editor to open the file and write the following lines:

```
<?php
phpinfo();
?>
```

If in the browser you enter the IP address of your Raspberry Pi followed by /infophp.php (192.168.XX / phpinfo.php), the corresponding page should appear. If so, you have set PHP correctly on your Raspberry Pi.

Set up MySQL

Setting up MySQL, set up the web server database through the command.

- sudo apt-get install php5-MySQL MySQL-server MySQL-client

Install everything you need. Immediately afterwards, you are asked to choose a root password for MySQL. Once this step is done and the database configuration is finished, complete the installation by restarting MySQL (using the Sudo /etc/init.d/mysql restart command) or the Raspberry Pi (using the sudo reboot command).

Set phpMyAdmin

To administer a MySQL database, you can use phpMyAdmin. With the help of this free software, you manage the database easily through a graphical user interface in the browser. To install, run this command line:

- sudo apt-get install PHPMyAdmin

In the screen that appears, choose Apache 2 as a web server. Here you are asked if the phpMyAdmin database management program should be installed, proceed by confirming. At this point, you still have to choose a password for phpMyAdmin (it can be the same one used for MySQL), and the installation will then be completed.

Finally, you have to connect the just installed phpMyAdmin with the Apache webserver. Execute the following command, through which you can modify the apache2. Conf configuration file from the editor:

- sudo nano /etc/apache2/apache2.conf

Now place the cursor at the end of the configuration file (to do this you can also press the key combination "CTRL" + "V" together) and write a new line here in the file:

- Include /etc/phpmyadmin/apache.conf

Now save the changes using the keyboard shortcuts "CTRL" + "O" and close the configuration file with "CTRL" + "X". Then restart the Apache webserver by entering the following command in the console:

- /etc/init.d/apache2 restart

Now you have configured the web server, and you can also manage your database directly from the browser via phpMyAdmin. Here, enter the IP address of the Raspberry Pi in the address bar followed by / PHPMyAdmin (192.168.XX / phpmyadmin) and log in on the page with the username "root" and the MySQL password chosen before. As soon as you have logged in, you can list the data on phpMyAdmin, create databases and tables or delete them, but also use other functions.

Using the webserver on the Raspberry Pi

Your web server is now configured and ready for use. For example, you can create and manage a site by inserting HTML and PHP pages on your web server. Create the individual pages directly on the Raspberry Pi to the / var/www (in Raspbian Wheezy) or / var/www / html (in Raspbian Jessie) or still prepare the pages on an external computer with an editor of your choice and transfer them after on the web server via an SFTP client, such as FileZilla, WinSCP, PuTTY or OpenSSH.

You can change the Apache webserver settings from the .htaccess configuration file. For example, create a 404 error page customized for your site or set up a redirection to another domain.

In addition to managing a site, a web server can be used for many other purposes. Thus it is possible to use the Raspberry Pi web server as a private file server or media server, or you can also set up a Cloud with the ownCloud free software and manage it. The file-sharing program allows you, among other things, to create files in the Cloud, to open and synchronize them. The list of projects that can be implemented with a web server on the Raspberry Pi is long: with your web server, you can now do what you want and achieve everything you want.

Web server security

Surely you have to pay attention to the security of the webserver. Especially if a server is constantly connected to the network, it is likely that attacks will occur sooner or later. Therefore it is mandatory always to guard your web server with the new updates and do not make them accumulate. Above all, you should handle sensitive data on a web server only once you are sure of everything you need to pay attention to in similar circumstances.

Configure a mail server with the Raspberry Pi to manage e-mails

Problems with the IP address of a private mail server

Before starting to set up a mail server on the Raspberry Pi, you should keep in mind that, generally, an e-mail server set up on its own does not equally replace a commercial one offered by a provider. This is due to the fact that most Internet connections do not have a static IP address. In order to use a mail server, an Internet connection is required. A more professional e-mail server uses an Internet connection, which uses at least one static (fixed) IP address, thus guaranteeing the server's constant reachability, since the address for Internet access remains unchanged.

As mentioned before, most connections are based only on a dynamic IP and this means that the address changes continuously (usually every 24 hours). This fact greatly limits the sending of messages with one's own mail server, because the recipient's e-mail server often classifies messages sent using a connection with a dynamic IP address as spam. This is also due to the fact that those who generate spam often use dynamic IPs to send his annoying messages, so you should try to avoid using a continuously changing address. Furthermore, e-mails that are automatically sent by a computer and have a dynamic IP are often not generated by the legitimate owner of the computer, but they are malware that has infiltrated the system.

Many spam mail server filters classify dynamic IP addresses as untrustworthy, for the reasons explained above. Therefore a connection to the Internet with a dynamic IP is only suitable in certain circumstances for sending messages via a connected mail server.

Even the email server presented in this tutorial, does not appear in this light as a classic email servers. However, with some additional measures and/or monthly costs it can be updated and transformed into a conventional mail server.

Advantages and disadvantages: when is it better to configure one's own mail server?

The difficulties that arise with a dynamic IP address represent the most serious flaw of a manually configured mail server. We therefore advise against using this server for daily e-mail traffic, as there is a risk that most of your messages will end up in the recipient's spam folder. But, even if the mail server does not replace your classic e-mail service, it may still be useful to set one.

If you are particularly interested in studying the configuration and administration of a mail server, surely it is more than appropriate to configure your own. For this there is no better way to learn at affordable prices than using a Raspberry Pi. It is also advisable to set up your own mail server, if in an internal network (for example a company or an organization) you would like to have absolute control over the data of your e-mails. A mail server in a local network ensures that the information exchanged is saved only on the sender's and recipient's hard drives and on your e-mail server.

Now more and more value is given to one's own privacy and therefore by setting up an internal mail server one has a secure solution available for saving one's messages, away from prying eyes. Thus only network administrators have access to the complete e-mail archive and sending does not take place via a provider's mail server. In the following paragraphs, we list in detail the pros and cons of configuring your own mail server with Raspberry Pi.

Advantages

In a private network only you have access to the complete e-mail archive. The messages are only found on your server, where third parties can read the emails only with your consent and in accordance with the right to privacy.

Even outside of a private network, it is possible to prevent third parties from accessing your e-mails, but for this reason the sender and the recipient need a private mail server. If the recipient in turn has an e-mail server configured and managed independently, without relying on any provider, all the data exchanged will be saved exclusively on the respective private mail servers.

It is advisable to use e-mail encryption techniques to protect your data, and this should be done even if e-mail traffic occurs between two private mail servers. As regards to data security, an autonomously managed mail server offers a further advantage: if e-mail is sent via the server of one or more providers. This can always read the header data of the messages, even if sender and recipient use PGP encryption. In fact, the data always remains open with the PGP software, but if both parties set up their own mail server, will avoid this privacy problem, keeping their message exchange private and not accessible to third parties.

Check the system on your own without exceptions and you can therefore configure the settings of the mail server software as you prefer. Furthermore you have no limitations regarding the size of the attachments or the general memory quota of your e-mail accounts (provided you have enough space to connect to the mail server).

You can synchronize your data (such as e-mail via IMAP, contacts via CardDAV or the calendar via CalDAV), so that the same data is present on all devices that access the mail server.

For the domain connected to the mail server you can create several e-mail addresses.

You do not receive any e-mail advertising from the provider.

Disadvantages

Managing one's own server involves greater responsibilities on the security front and a mail server is certainly no exception, since it remains permanently online and can always be a victim of hacker attacks. You should regularly update the software, in particular the data protection programs and check them, so that hackers cannot access your server (and possibly use it to send spam emails). To administer a mail server accessible to the public, one must therefore be well informed about security standards and always keep up to date.

As already mentioned, outgoing e-mails that have a dynamic IP address are most likely seen by the recipient's mail server as spam and end up directly in the appropriate folder. But it is possible to circumvent the inconvenience in these two ways:

To send e-mails use another mail server (commercial), on which you already have an e-mail address. Once you have finished configuring your mail server, you can set up a connected e-mail client, through which you send messages from the provider's server and not yours.

Disadvantage: the process is at the expense of full control over your data. In fact the service of the provider is activated and the outgoing messages are saved on its server, where it is also possible to read them.

Request a static IP address for your connection. So your private mail server will get much closer to the professional ones, although it is not unlikely that the static address will first have to gain a certain reputation among the other servers (and therefore prove to be reliable with other providers). Many mail servers are in fact skeptical, in case they receive messages from new mail servers. First of all, you must prove that your server is not being used for sending spam.

In order to effectively manage your own mail server, in addition to a static IP address, you should still have:

a Mail Exchange Resource Record (abbreviated as MX Record) of the domain in use. It is a resource of the Domain Name System (DNS), which reports your mail server as a server assigned to receive emails on a specific domain

PTR Resource Record (PTR Record), which through "reverse lookup" of the DNS, goes back from the IP address to the associated host name.

However, a connection to the Internet with a static IP address is not always easy to obtain, and in the event that you are able to obtain it, it usually involves higher costs.

The spam filters of private mail servers are less effective than those of the most popular providers, as their software has already learned a lot from the enormous quantity of processed e-mails, thus managing to better identify spam e-mails and classify them. However, it is possible to improve the protection against spam on your mail server through specific programs.

Requirements for configuring your own mail server

First of all you obviously need an e-mail address to freely dispose of. For this you register a domain and as you will most likely have (as usual) a dynamic IP address, we explain below how to install a mail server on your Raspberry Pi with an IP of this type.

To configure a mail server on Raspberry Pi, in addition to this small computer, you will also need:

- of the Raspbian operating system;
- of a memory card (micro) SD (at least 4GB of space, but better if more);

- a flat Internet connection (connected with a network cable or even via Wi-Fi);

- of a constant supply of the current necessary for the Raspberry Pi (via micro-USB);

- of a computer with SSH client (like PuTTY or OpenSSH), connected to the Raspberry Pi (here just enter the IP address of the Raspberry Pi in the SSH client), to make remote access to the Raspberry Pi terminal

or

- of a screen and input devices to use the terminal, if you do not want to use the SSH client.

You can also use another memory medium (like a pen drive or an external hard disk), in case you need more space on the mail server.

A mail server must always be reachable on the Internet at the same address and therefore it is necessary to be constantly online. Also for this reason, a static IP address is the best solution for your connection, but often not available. Alternatively you can also use services, which offer (often for free) a dynamic DNS (DDNS). Use DDNS to assign a domain name to your mail server. With the help of a program, this domain name is associated with the current IP address of your connection and thus becomes a fixed address of your mail server. Some routers have already integrated a similar function, for example those of Fritz! Box (find out more about how to set up a DDNS for your mail server on the official website of the product.

Configure a mail server on Raspberry Pi

Before switching to the actual mail server configuration, establish a static private IP address within the network for the Raspberry Pi. A mail server is controlled in the same way as a website through an IP address on the network and to be always reachable by all mail servers, the server needs to keep the same address. This fixed IP address of the local network is not to be confused with that of the Internet connection, which was discussed earlier.

Establish a private static IP address

In your local network a Raspberry Pi mail server needs a static IP address to be able to manage all incoming and outgoing e-mails at any time. But since a Raspberry Pi is normally assigned a dynamic IP address in a local network, you must now assign it a static IP address.

To change the local IP of the Raspberry Pi, you must first identify the current dynamic IP, for example by scrolling the mouse over the Internet symbol on the desktop of the Raspbian operating system. Write down this address. In our tutorial we take for example our original dynamic IP address 192.168.0.3 for the Raspberry Pi.

After clicking with the right mouse button on the Internet symbol, select the option Wi-Fi options and, on the appeared menu, click on "eth0". In the appropriate field enter the sequence of numbers (each three-digit block separated by a dot) of the IP address, in our example 192.168.0. Now add in the last field one digit, which has not been assigned to any other device on the network (in general, all the numbers above 100 are reserved for static IP addresses). In our tutorial we use the IP address 192.168.0.101. After establishing the static private IP address, restart the Raspberry Pi.

Install the mail server with Citadel/UX on the Raspberry Pi

In the next step you should configure the mail server on the Raspberry Pi. In this case we use the Citadel/UX groupware, which supports the SMTP protocol as well as IMAP and POP3. In addition, Citadel comes with the user interface of a webmail and also offers functions for calendaring, managing contacts and notes.

For the configuration use the terminal and from there update the packages already installed with the following commands:

- sudo apt-get update
- sudo apt-get upgrade

Citadel is preconfigured to use IPv4 and IPv6 addresses as transfer protocols during installation. As soon as the program realizes that no IPv6 can be used, the installation process is interrupted. Therefore activate the protocol with the command

- sudo modprobe ipv6

and then configure Citadel with this string:

- sudo apt-get install citadel-suite

On the next screen, set the server to receive requests on all addresses, accepting the default address 0.0.0.0. Other commands follow, through which you can decide to use an internal database to manage the Citadel password. Also choose the administrator user name (here you can simply leave "admin", as proposed) and the related password.

At this point you have to choose whether to use Citadel with the internal Webcit web server (already included in the groupware) or if you want to connect the already installed Apache web server, certainly the right solution if you have already followed our tutorial and configured an Apache web server on the Raspberry Pi. Below we explain how to configure an internal web server and we assume that you have chosen to use the usual ports offered for the mail server (configure port forwarding for HTTP port 80 and 443 HTTPS port). Finally, set the language for the Webcit web server.

Configure the mail server with Citadel

Now start Citadel from the terminal with this command:

- sudo service citadel start

Then on your browser enter the static private IP address of your Raspberry Pi (in our example 192.168.0.101), so as to open the Citadel mail server. However, you can't log in to the program yet, as you still have to set Citadel to not access via IPv6, but via IPv4.

For this use the terminal again and start the Citadel setup again with the command

- sudo /usr/lib/citadel-server/setup

Log in as admin. Keep the username " citadel " and enter 0.0.0.0 as the address again; you can leave the remaining setup settings as they are. Finally, to save all changes, restart Citadel.

Connect the mail server with Citadel on the Raspberry Pi

If you open Citadel again from the browser, entering the IP address of the Raspberry Pi, you should now also be able to log in with the username admin and the related password. First choose from the side menu on the left "Administration" and click on "Global configuration" under "Change system settings". In this tutorial, we will only set the Simple Mail Transfer Protocol (SMTP), necessary for sending e-mails; IMAP and POP3 configuration to receive and open e-mails must be done in a similar way.

Select the "SMTP" menu item. Here you see the three ports used by the Citadel mail server. In order to use them, however, you must make sure that your router is also unlocked. So mark the numbers of the three ports and configure your router accordingly.

In case you do not know your address, enter the command "ipconfig" in the Windows command prompt and check the address marked under "Default gateway"; most of the time it is 192.168.0.1 or 192.168.178.1. Log in now on the router configuration page. If you have never set a custom username or have never changed your initial password, go to RouterPasswords.comfind many models and their default settings. As soon as you are on the router configuration settings, go to the port forwarding menu. Here, enter the IP address of the Raspberry Pi, including the numbers of the three ports. Furthermore, you still need to set port 80 for the interface of your webmail. Once all these steps are finished, you can use Citadel as a mail server.

Connect the domain name with the IP address of the mail server

To make the Raspberry Pi mail server always reachable at the same address, register with a DDNS service, enter the corresponding domain name there and connect it to Citadel in the last step. You must register the domain name as " DNS Host (A) " by providing your current IP address, which your provider has assigned to you. You can find out what this IP address is for example on www.whatsmyip.org

If you enter the domain name registered in your browser, a page of your Citadel mail server opens. Now you have to open the menu item "Administration" and click on "Configuration of the domain name and e-mail". Here enter and add the domain name to the "alias for this machine" entry. Finally go to "Change system settings" under "Administration". Here you first delete the "node name" and enter your domain name in its place under "Fully qualified domain name". Once you have saved the settings, click again on the "Administration" menu item and choose to restart the Citadel mail server.

Now everything is ready: your mail server is configured and can be used via the installed webmail. You can also use it with another email client (Thunderbird, Outlook, etc.) and expand Citadel with many other functions.

Conclusion: when is it advisable to configure a mail server on a Raspberry Pi?

If you use the Raspberry Pi as a mail server together with an Internet connection with a static IP address, you can set up a professional e-mail server. In this case it is advisable to enter not only the mandatory fields mentioned above (PTR Record and MX Record), but also SPF Resource Record (SPF Record) and DKIM (DomainKeys). Thus you reduce the possibility of other servers classifying outgoing emails from your mail server as spam. Obviously, as already mentioned, a mail server must first build its own reputation, so that the messages sent are classified less and less as spam, a practice difficult to reach with private servers where few activities are recorded.

If you only have an Internet connection with a dynamic IP address, to make it work better, you can configure the Raspberry Pi mail server via DDNS, even if your e-mails will often end up in the recipient's spam folder. Therefore it is important to inform the main recipients of your messages to configure the spam filter, so that your emails do not end up as spam. It is advisable to give a similar warning if you want to reach a specific group of people (such as colleagues in the company, a work group, etc.) with the mail server. But above all, if all the participants are connected to the same local network, it is certainly worth configuring an internal mail server.

One of the major advantages of configuring your own mail server without connecting to a provider lies in absolute data control. If it is not so important for you to set up and manage your own mail server for this reason, it is unlikely that you will be rewarded for the considerable effort required for configuring, checking and updating the server. In such a case, it is best to consult a large e-mail provider. In general, to take advantage of a private mail server, it is mainly the technicians of the sector and the enthusiasts, who would like to know and understand the technology behind a mail server using the Raspberry Pi.